W9-ABU-048
R00815 74901

by

Anne & Harlow Rockwell

Macmillan Publishing Company

New York

 Macmillan Publishing Company, 866 Third Avenue, New York, N.Y. 10022. Collier Macmillan Canada, Inc. Library of Congress catalog card number: 72-185149 Printed in the United States of America.
ISBN 0-02-777520-8 6 7 8 9 10

The pictures in this book are full-color watercolor paintings. The typeface is Futura Medium, hand set.

for Oliver

Machines work.

We use

machines.

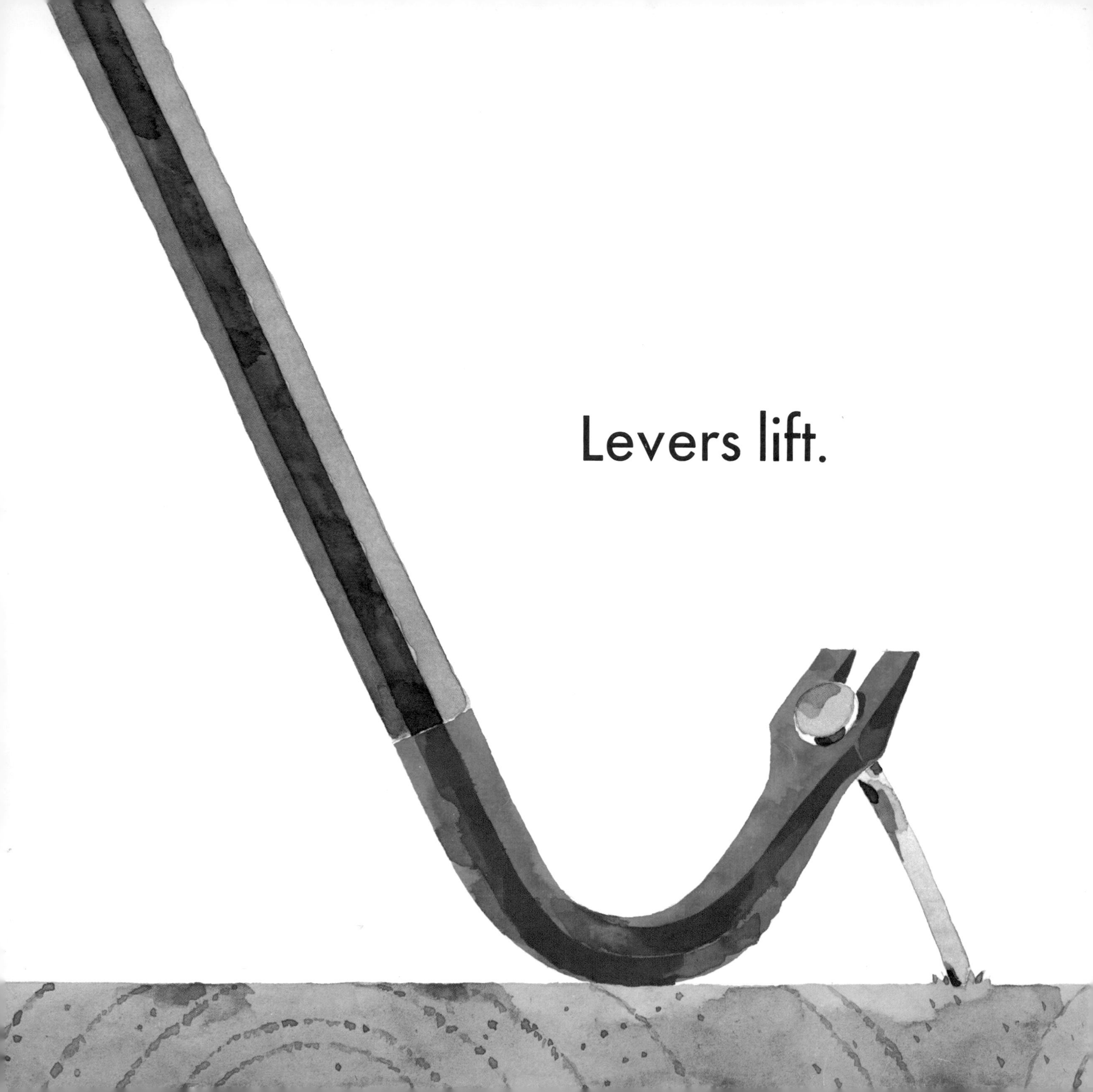

Levers lift.

Wheels turn.

A pulley is a wheel
with a groove
for a rope.

A block and tackle
to pull things up
is made of pulleys.

A gear is a wheel with teeth
that turn another gear.

Ball bearings make wheels turn smoothly.

A jackscrew raises heavy things.

Sprockets on a wheel
grip holes in a chain.
They pull the chain
around and around.

Fuel makes some

machines work.

Electricity makes
other machines work.

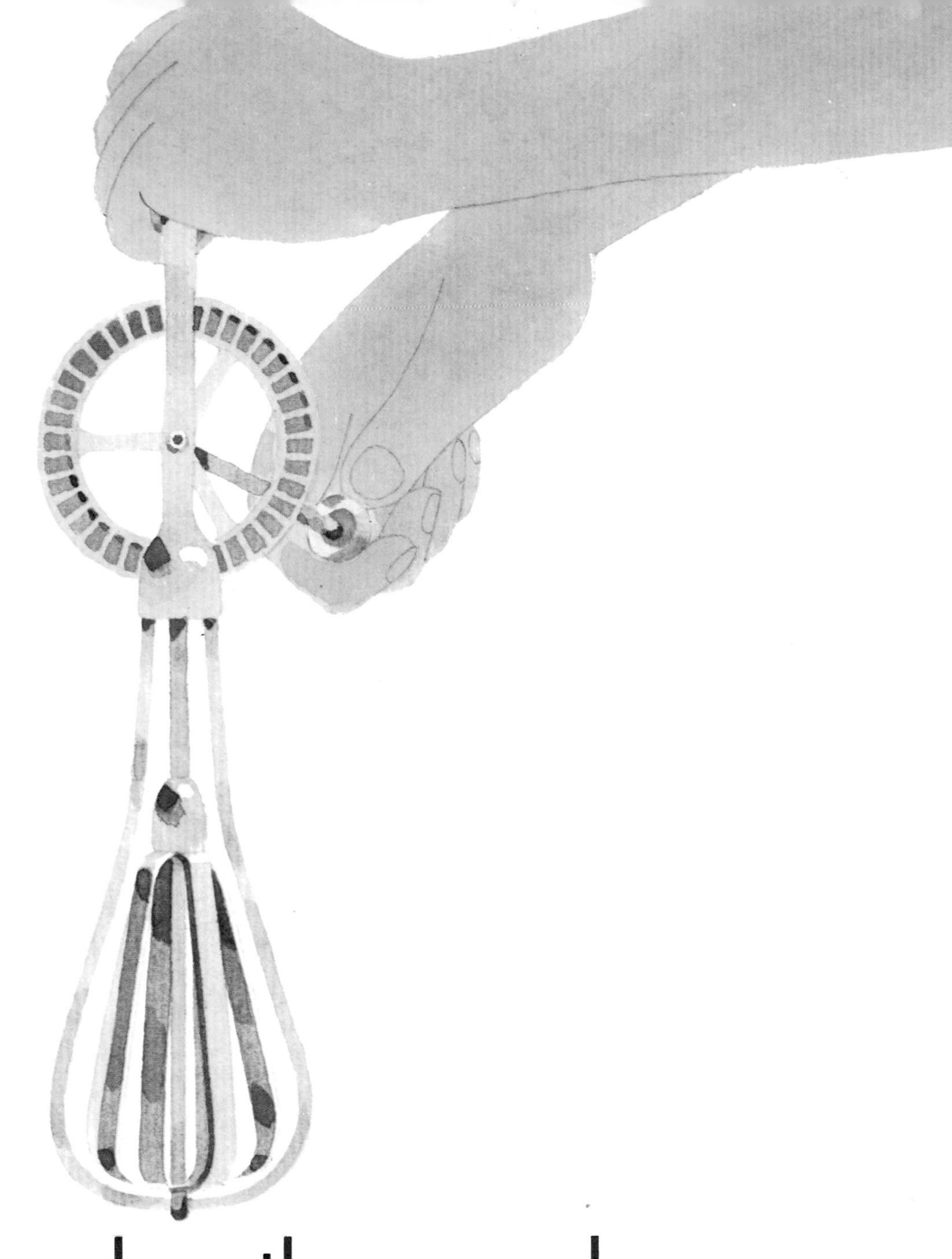

Hands make others work.

My bicycle is a machine.
My feet make it work.

There are many machines
that do many things.

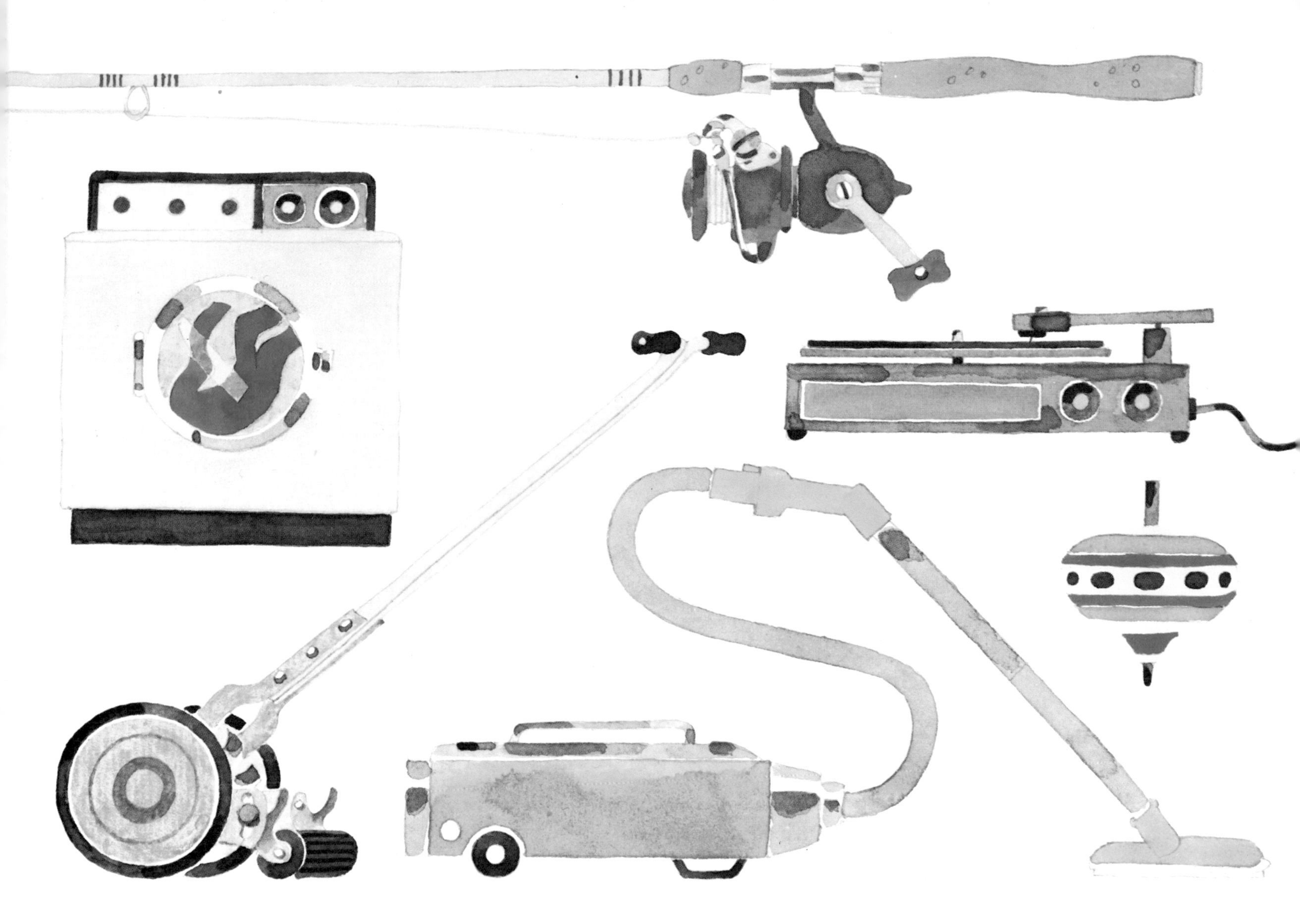

I like machines.